Ed Robb &

THE Wonder
OF CHRISTMAS

ONCE YOU BELIEVE, ANYTHING IS POSSIBLE

Leader Guide
by Lori Jones

Abingdon Press / Nashville

THE WONDER OF CHRISTMAS
ONCE YOU BELIEVE, ANYTHING IS POSSIBLE
LEADER GUIDE

This book is printed on elemental chlorine-free paper.
ISBN 978-1-5018-2325-1

Some material has been excerpted from The Wonder of Christmas, Ed Robb and Rob Renfroe (Nashville: Abingdon Press, 2016). Page references are noted within parentheses.

16 17 18 19 20 21 22 23 24 25 — 10 9 8 7 6 5 4 3 2 1
MANUFACTURED IN THE UNITED STATES OF AMERICA

Contents

To the Leader

Christmas is the story of a star shining brightly, a name declared joyfully, a manger waiting expectantly, and a promise given freely. Yes, it is the story of what happened on a bright, starlit night some two thousand years ago in the village of Bethlehem, but it is also the story of what is happening right now, right where you are. Without Christmas we could never fully know the wonder of God's love.

The wonder of Christmas is that God loved us more than we could imagine and came to live among us so that we could experience God with us. *The Wonder of Christmas* walks us through the four weeks of Advent, exploring four elements of the Christmas story that teach us about the wonder of God's great love for us:

- The Wonder of a Star
- The Wonder of a Name
- The Wonder of a Manger
- The Wonder of a Promise

As we look to the Christmas story and consider our own stories in the process, we will rediscover that the true wonder of Christmas is found in the love of Christ and made real in our hearts when we share that love with others.

The season of Advent invites us to see the world through the gift of wonder. It is an invitation to look for the beauty in what God has done and believe there is more to this world than what we can see or understand; to be amazed by the most wonderful story ever told, a story that continues through each of our lives. You are invited to enter this season with a spirit of curiosity, asking the Lord to astonish you anew.

How to Facilitate This Study

This four-session small group study makes use of the following components:

- *The Wonder of Christmas* book
- this Leader Guide
- *The Wonder of Christmas* DVD

Additional resources for children, youth, and worship are available for making the study a church-wide emphasis during Advent.

You will want to distribute copies of *The Wonder of Christmas* to the members of your group in advance, communicating that they are to read the Introduction and Chapter 1 *before* your first group session. As you gather each week, you will have the opportunity to watch a video, discuss and respond to what you're learning, and pray together. In addition to some basic supplies (refer to each session outline for a list of materials needed), you will need a DVD player or computer, and a television or projection screen for watching the DVD segments as part of your group session. You also will need an Advent wreath for the closing activity.

To create a warm and inviting atmosphere for your group session and to connect with the study's theme of the wonder of Christmas, you might consider hanging Christmas lights in your meeting space or decorating a small Christmas tree with beautiful ornaments and lights. Though optional, you also might consider serving Christmas cookies as refreshments.

In this book you will find outlines for four group sessions, each structured for a 60-minute format. (For a longer session, choose from the "Additional Material" provided at the end of the session outline.) Each session plan includes the following:

Planning for the Session

For your planning prior to the group session, this section provides goals for the session, a list of materials needed, and steps for preparation. Be sure to review this section, as well as the session outline, before your group gathers. If you choose, you also may find it helpful to review the DVD segment in advance.

Getting Started (10 minutes)

Each session begins with an opening activity followed by prayer. You may want to pray your own prayer or invite a participant to pray. Or if you prefer, you may use the printed prayer provided for each session.

Content Review (40 minutes)

Following the opening activity and prayer, watch the week's video segment together (approximately 10–12 minutes). Then use the discussion points and questions to explore material from the book and video (approximately 25–28 minutes). You may choose to read this material aloud or summarize it in your own words. If you would like to utilize other material in your session or are planning a longer session, choose from the "Additional Material" found after the closing prayer.

Closing (10 minutes)

End each session by lighting an Advent wreath, announcing the "Watching for Wonder" weekly challenge, and closing with prayer (use either the printed prayer or offer one of your own).

Before You Begin

You are encouraged to personalize this study by modifying or adapting the session outlines and activities to match your teaching style and/or to meet the needs and interests of your group. No one knows your group better than you do. As you plan for each session, be sure to make prayer a part of your weekly preparation. Pray for every group member by name, for each session, and for God to work in and through you as you lead the group.

May you grow in faith and hope as you open yourselves anew to the wonder of Christmas!

Helpful Hints

Preparing for Each Session

- Pray for wisdom and discernment from the Holy Spirit, for you and for each member of the group, as you prepare for the study.
- Before each session, familiarize yourself with the content. Read the book chapter and review the session outline.
- Choose the session elements you will use during the group session, including the specific discussion questions you plan to cover. Be prepared, however, to adjust the session as group members interact and questions arise. Prepare carefully, but allow space for the Holy Spirit to move in and through the group members and through you as facilitator.
- Prepare the space where the group will meet so that the space will enhance the learning process. Ideally, group members should be seated around a table or in a circle so that all can see one another. Movable chairs are best so that the group easily can form pairs or small groups for discussion.

Shaping the Learning Environment

- Create a climate of openness, encouraging group members to participate as they feel comfortable.
- Remember that some people will jump right in with answers and comments, while others need time to process what is being discussed.
- If you notice that some group members seem never to be able to enter the conversation, ask them if they have thoughts to share. Give everyone a chance to talk, but keep the conversation moving. Moderate to prevent a few individuals from doing all the talking.
- Communicate the importance of group discussions and group exercises.
- If no one answers at first during discussions, do not be afraid of silence. Count silently to ten, then say something such as, "Would anyone like to go first?" If no one responds, venture an answer yourself and ask for comments.
- Model openness as you share with the group. Group members will follow your example. If you limit your sharing to a surface level, others will follow suit.
- Encourage multiple answers or responses before moving on.
- Ask, "Why?" or "Why do you believe that?" or "Can you say more about that?" to help continue a discussion and give it greater depth.
- Affirm others' responses with comments such as "Great" or "Thanks" or "Good insight"—especially if it's the first time someone has spoken during the group session.
- Monitor your own contributions. If you are doing most of the talking, back off so that you do not train the group to listen rather than speak up.
- Remember that you do not have all the answers. Your job is to keep the discussion going and encourage participation.

Managing the Session

- Honor the time schedule. If a session is running longer than expected, get consensus from the group before continuing beyond the agreed-upon ending time.
- Involve group members in various aspects of the group session, such as saying prayers or reading Scripture aloud.
- Note that the session guides sometimes call for breaking into smaller groups or pairs. This gives everyone a chance to speak and participate fully. Mix up the groups; don't let the same people pair up for every activity.
- As always in discussions that may involve personal sharing, confidentiality is essential. Group members should never pass along stories that have been shared in the group. Remind the group members at each session of the importance of confidentiality.

Session 1

The Wonder of a Star

Planning for the Session

Session Goals

Participants will be encouraged to:

- Discover ways to be awakened to the wonder of Christmas.
- Think about ways in which we pursue *more* in our lives, and what is behind that desire.
- Consider how the birth of Jesus fulfills our hopes.
- Ask the Lord how we should follow and be aware of the meaning of this season.

Materials Needed

- *The Wonder of Christmas* book (one for every participant)
- Bibles (extras for participants)

- *The Wonder of Christmas DVD*, DVD player
- Markerboard or chart paper, markers
- Advent wreath, candles, matches

Optional:

- Writing paper or journals, pens or pencils for journaling (provide or have participants bring their own)
- Recordings of Christmas carols or hymns
- Inexpensive or homemade star ornaments (one for each participant)

Preparation

- Read and reflect on Chapter 1, "The Wonder of a Star."
- Read through the session outline and select the material you plan to cover.
- Read and reflect on the following scriptures:
  o Genesis 1
  o Isaiah 43:1
  o Ecclesiastes 3:11
  o Psalm 42:7-8
  o Isaiah 55:2
  o Matthew 4:18-22
  o Matthew 14:22-33
- Prepare the room and gather the necessary materials. Cue the video for Session 1. Be sure to set out an Advent wreath to light during the closing. (Don't forget matches!) You may want to play some soft Christmas music during this time. If you choose, you may have participants journal during this time.
- *Optional:* Make or purchase inexpensive star ornaments (one for each participant) to hand out during the closing.

Getting Started (10 minutes)

Opening Activity

Welcome participants as they arrive. Open your time together by discussing the following questions:

- Can you recall a time when you eagerly hoped and waited for a specific Christmas gift? Describe the gift and if you received it. (If time permits, you could have each member anonymously write down what the gift was on a slip of paper; then draw them out one by one and try to guess who wanted each gift.)
- Advent is a time of waiting and reflection. What do you hope to experience this Advent?

Opening Prayer

Lord, as we begin this study, we thank you for the opportunity to slow down and spend these weeks contemplating the joy and wonder of the greatest gift we've ever been given—Jesus Christ. As we reflect on the Christmas story and the questions it raises, speak to us and make us aware of the grand story you are telling and how we fit into it. Thank you for your abundant love and mercy. Now bless our time together as we seek you this season. In Jesus' name. Amen.

Content Review and Application (40 minutes)

Note: This section allows approximately 10–12 minutes for a video segment and 25–28 minutes for discussion. More content has been provided than you will have time to cover. Select in advance those questions you would like to discuss, putting a check mark beside each one.

Video

Play Session 1 (running time 11:24).

Discuss:

- When have you experienced a longing for "something more"? In what ways has this longing led you to seek after God?

- What are some of the "signs" in your life that have pointed you to God?
- Why does it require real courage to go to Jesus?

Study and Discussion (25–28 minutes)

The Gift of Wonder

Read aloud or summarize:

Do you know someone who seems to notice things that others don't—who pays attention to the subtle details and finds beauty and meaning in the unexpected? Maybe it's you!

Rob Renfroe writes, "As we explore the wonder of Christmas together in the coming weeks, you are invited to see the world—and what God has done—through the gift of wonder; to believe there is more to this world than the eye beholds; to look for the beauty in what God has done and allow yourself to be amazed by a story you've heard a hundred times; to come to this season with a spirit of curiosity, trusting that if you will slow down and open your heart, Creation's Artist will astonish you with gifts that are waiting for you" (pp. 16-17).

Discuss:

- Each of us enters the Christmas season with expectations about what this year's celebration will be like. How do past Christmases shape or influence how you feel about Christmas this year?
- What does *wonder* mean to you? Who or what causes you to wonder—to be amazed, curious, or inspired?
- Take turns reading aloud Genesis 1, the story of creation. How does meditating on this story affect your view of God and inspire wonder in your heart?

The Search for More

Read aloud or summarize:

> After Jesus was born in Bethlehem in Judea, during
> the time of King Herod, Magi from the east came to
> Jerusalem and asked, "Where is the one who has been
> born king of the Jews? We saw his star when it rose and
> have come to worship him."...
>
> They went on their way, and the star they had seen
> when it rose went ahead of them until it stopped over
> the place where the child was. When they saw the star,
> they were overjoyed. On coming to the house, they saw
> the child with his mother Mary, and they bowed down
> and worshiped him. Then they opened their treasures
> and presented him with gifts of gold, frankincense and
> myrrh." (Matthew 2:1-2, 9-11)

The story of the wise men is familiar to anyone who has ever heard
the biblical Christmas story. The magi had "successful" lives in terms
of what the world values. They didn't need more money or accolades.
So why did they put aside everything to go and follow a star? What
compelled them to travel hundreds of miles through barren terrain
and unknown dangers to find a promised king? What did they hope to
gain? What did they long to find?

At one time or another, all of us sense that we are made for more.
We ask questions and go on journeys to find the answers. Often we feel
that something is missing—that we need something more in order for
our lives to be right. But not all of us recognize what this need for more
truly is. In fact, many people who yearn for more end up focusing on
simply getting more of the same—more wealth, more success, more
recognition, more possessions, more pleasure—more of everything
that has already left them unsatisfied and unfulfilled.

Discuss:

- What do you think the magi were looking for when they set out to find Jesus?
- In what ways do people in our society tend to spend time and resources searching for *more*?
- Read the following verses aloud. How do they speak to this deep yearning of our hearts for something *more?*

> *Deep calls to deep / in the roar of your waterfalls; / all your waves and breakers / have swept over me. / By day the LORD directs his love, / at night his song is with me—/ a prayer to the God of my life. (Psalm 42:7-8)*

> *He has made everything beautiful in its time. He has also set eternity in the human heart; yet no one can fathom what God has done from beginning to end.*
> *(Ecclesiastes 3:11)*

> *"I have called you by name. You are Mine!"*
> *(Isaiah 43:1 NLV)*

> *"Why spend money on what is not bread, / and your labor on what does not satisfy? / Listen, listen to me, and eat what is good, / and you will delight in the richest of fare." (Isaiah 55:2)*

- The longing within us is a yearning for something more than this world can provide; we long for our Savior. As Saint Augustine wrote, "Thou hast made us for thyself, and restless is our heart until it comes to rest in thee."[1] How have you found this to be true in your own life?

Stars and Signs and Prophets

Read aloud or summarize:

The wise men saw the star for what it was—a sign from God. They had been paying attention, and when the sign came, they followed. But long before the star appeared in the sky above the town of Bethlehem, God was sending signs to his people to tell them of Jesus' birth. Since the beginning, when he created Adam and Eve, God had been speaking to his people, reminding them of who they were and whose they were. Even when things were bleak and the future seemed very dim, God spoke to his people again and again, reminding them of the Savior to come. Let's read about some of these Old Testament prophecies and how they were fulfilled in the New Testament.

Activity:

Ask one member of your group to play the part of prophet and read aloud the Old Testament prophecies below. After the prophet reads each prophecy, have another group member answer that prophecy by reading aloud the New Testament fulfillment:

Old Testament Prophecy	**New Testament Fulfillment**
Isaiah 7:14	Matthew 1:18-23
Micah 5:2	Matthew 2:1
Isaiah 9:1-2	Matthew 4:12-16
Isaiah 61:1-2	Luke 4:16-19
Isaiah 53:5-12	Romans 5:6-8

Discuss:

- How were these prophecies fulfilled in the New Testament? What might the fulfillment of these prophecies have meant to people in ancient Israel? How can these prophecies affect our modern-day thinking about Jesus?

The Call to Follow

Read aloud or summarize:

The wise men had the courage to follow the star. Mary and Joseph had the courage to accept the Lord's plan for them, even though it turned their lives upside down. But many who heard about Jesus'

19

birth, such as Herod and others in Jerusalem, chose to stay home and continue their everyday lives as if nothing had changed.

Why didn't they go too? They were familiar with the prophecy; they knew this was no small event. Could it have been that they were afraid of what they would find? After all, if the Messiah had truly come into the world as had been prophesied, things were about to change; perhaps those in power knew Jesus' birth meant that they would have to change too.

An encounter with Jesus demands a response from us—will we accept his call, or will we stay home?

Discuss:

- Read aloud Matthew 4:18-22 about Jesus calling his first disciples to come and walk with him. Imagine the scene as Jesus calls out to these men. Notice the Bible says they respond immediately. Why do you think they go so quickly without hesitating?
- Read aloud the story about Jesus and Peter, found in Matthew 14:22-33. Peter follows Jesus' call wholeheartedly at first but then gets distracted and hesitates. What is Jesus' response?
- Have you ever sensed Jesus calling you? How did you respond?

Closing (10 minutes)

Lighting the Advent Wreath

Present the Advent wreath and prepare to light the first candle. You might dim the lights or play some soft background music during this time, possibly some traditional Christmas hymns such as "O Little Town of Bethlehem" and "Come, Thou Long-Expected Jesus."

Read aloud or summarize:

In many of our churches and homes, we mark the four weeks before Christmas using an Advent wreath—a circular wreath of evergreen leaves that symbolizes the eternity of God. The wreath typically features four candles representing Hope, Peace, Love, and Joy. We light one candle each week of Advent as we await Jesus' coming. We place the fifth candle, the Christ candle, in the middle of the wreath and light it on Christmas Day to celebrate Jesus' birth.

This week, the first week of Advent, we light the candle of Hope and reflect on the wonder of the star placed high above Bethlehem, sent as a sign from God to announce the fulfillment of our deepest hopes and dreams—the birth of Immanuel, God with us.

- Spend about five minutes in silence together, prompting the group to pray that God would open our eyes this season to the gift of wonder. Encourage them to ask the Lord for specific ways they can limit distractions so that they are able to focus on him this Advent. If you choose, invite participants to journal during this time.
- *Optional:* If you made or purchased star ornaments for your group, give them out now as visual reminders of the star over Bethlehem and the wonder of the gift of Jesus. Encourage group members to place the stars on their trees or other places in their homes or workplaces during Advent.

Watching for Wonder Challenge

Encourage participants to be watching for unexpected gifts this week—evidences that there is more to this world than what the eye beholds; glimpses of God at work in the people, places, and circumstances of their daily lives. Invite them to journal about what they see or to share their thoughts with a family member or friend.

Closing Prayer

Heavenly Father, thank you for the gift of your Son—for sending him to be Immanuel, God with us. We praise you for all the ways you unexpectedly reveal yourself to us and ask that you open our eyes to see the wonder you have placed all around us during this season. Help us to be present and listen for your voice as we celebrate your coming.

Additional Material

Read the Christmas Story

Read aloud or summarize:

We have heard the Christmas story countless times—so often that we rarely read through the biblical story in its entirety. Take some time with your group now to do just that.

- Quiet the room and lead the group in prayer, asking the Lord to reveal something new to each person as you read aloud the story of Jesus' birth.
- Read aloud the following passages in this order (invite participants to take turns):
  o Luke 1:1-56
  o Matthew 1:18-25
  o Luke 2:1-21
  o Matthew 2:1-12
- Ask group members to share anything that God might have revealed to them as the story was read.

The Helper

Read aloud or summarize:

The Christmas story is full of unlikely elements—a star so bright it couldn't be ignored; a stable, the most unlikely place for the Son of God to be born; a group of farm laborers, the first to witness the newborn King.

Many things in life defy explanation or understanding. Thankfully, God doesn't leave us to figure out these mysteries on our own. As Jesus prepared his disciples for his death on the cross, he assured them that he would not leave them alone but would ask God the Father to send a helper, the Holy Spirit, to live within them and guide them along the way. This same Holy Spirit lives within each of us!

Discuss:

- Read aloud John 14:25-27. How do you imagine the disciples felt at hearing this news?

Read aloud or summarize:

God, in his infinite wisdom, did not leave us alone to rely on our own wisdom. Instead he sent the Holy Spirit to guide us. In God's great love for us, God declared: "You will seek me and find me when you seek me with all your heart. I will be found by you" (Jeremiah 29:13-14a). Even though life is full of mystery and wonder, God *wants* to be found by us—God wants to be in an intimate relationship with God's children.

Discuss:

- How does the Holy Spirit help us to find God? What evidence of this have you seen in your own life?

Session 2

The Wonder of a Name

Planning for the Session

Session Goals

Participants will be encouraged to:

- Explore the importance and purpose of the most important name in the Christmas story: Jesus.
- Meditate on the name of Jesus and what it means to those who believe in him.
- Discover our new identities and names as followers of Christ.

Materials Needed

- *The Wonder of Christmas* book (one for every participant)
- Bibles (extras for participants)
- *The Wonder of Christmas* DVD, DVD player

- Markerboard or chart paper, markers
- Two index cards or slips of paper for each participant
- Copies of the scriptures on page 34 (one for each participant)
- Advent wreath, candles, matches

Optional:
- Writing paper or journals, pens or pencils for journaling (provide or have participants bring their own)
- Recordings of Christmas carols or hymns

Preparation

- Read and reflect on Chapter 2, "The Wonder of a Name."
- Read through the session outline and select the material you plan to cover.
- Read and reflect on the following Scriptures:
  - o John 1:14
  - o Acts 5:31
  - o Ephesians 1:22-23
  - o Matthew 1:21
  - o Numbers 14:7-9
  - o John 1:9-13
  - o Romans 8:1-2
  - o Isaiah 43:1
- Prepare the room and gather the necessary materials. Cue the video for Session 2. Be sure to set out an Advent wreath to light during the closing. (Don't forget matches!) You may want to play some soft Christmas music during this time. If you choose, you may have participants journal during this time.

Getting Started (10 minutes)

Opening Activity

Welcome participants as they arrive. Begin the session with a word association exercise. Ask participants to brainstorm a list of names they associate with the Christmas season. Write these on a markerboard or chart paper. Responses likely will range from names of characters in the biblical Christmas story to those of secular characters such as Scrooge or Santa Claus. As time permits, choose several of the names and ask what words or descriptions come to mind for each.

Read aloud or summarize:

There is no doubt that names hold meaning and importance. Today we will explore the importance and purpose of the most important name in the Christmas story: Jesus.

Opening Prayer

Lord, thank you for another opportunity to gather together and study your Word. As we learn more about Jesus, help us to remember that you sent him to earth for us; he is our Rescuer and Redeemer. Open our hearts and minds to you and the words you have for us today. In Jesus' holy name. Amen.

Content Review and Application (40 minutes)

Note: This section allows approximately 10–12 minutes for a video segment and 25–28 minutes for discussion. More content has been provided than you will have time to cover. Select in advance those questions you would like to discuss, putting a check mark beside each one.

Video

Play Session 2 (running time 12:00).
Discuss:

- How is the name Jesus wonderful (wonder-filled) to you?
- How does understanding the name Jesus help to restore the true wonder of Christmas for you?
- What would it mean for you to "lean into" the wonder of the name Jesus this Christmas?

Study and Discussion (25–28 minutes)

Name Above All Names

Read aloud or summarize:

Long before his birth, people were talking about Jesus. Throughout the Bible we are told what Jesus' coming would mean for the world. Descriptions of him fill both the Old and the New Testaments. What can we learn about the name Jesus that can help to awaken us to the wonder of Christmas?

Listen for the names given for Jesus in these scriptures. (Have someone read aloud the following scriptures as you record the names given for Jesus—indicated below in bold type—on a markerboard or chart paper.)

> "For my eyes have seen your **salvation**, / which you have prepared in the sight of all nations: / a **light** for revelation to the Gentiles, / and **the glory of your people Israel**." *(Luke 2:30-32)*

> **The Word** *became flesh and made his dwelling among us. We have seen his glory, the glory of the one and only Son, who came from the Father, full of grace and truth. (John 1:14)*

> *[Jesus said,] "I am* **the good shepherd**. *The good shepherd lays down his life for the sheep." (John 10:11)*

> *God exalted him to his own right hand as* **Prince** *and* **Savior** *that he might bring Israel to repentance and forgive their sins. (Acts 5:31)*

> *God put everything under Christ's feet and made him* **head of everything in the church,** *which is his body. His body, the church, is the fullness of Christ, who fills everything in every way.*
>
> *(Ephesians 1:22-23 CEB)*

*Fixing our eyes on Jesus, the **pioneer and perfecter of faith**. For the joy set before him he endured the cross, scorning its shame, and sat down at the right hand of the throne of God.*

(Hebrews 12:2)

*There is one God and one **mediator** between God and humanity, the human Christ Jesus.*

(1 Timothy 2:5 CEB)

*"I am the **Alpha** and the **Omega**, the **Beginning** and the **End**, the **First** and the **Last**."*

(Revelation 22:13 NKJV)

Discuss:

- Scripture calls Jesus Light, the Word, Prince, Savior, Head of the church, Pioneer and Perfecter of faith, Mediator, First, and Last. Those who were with him called him Teacher, Healer, Prophet, King of the Jews, Messiah. What name of Jesus do you most identify with and why?
- How might choosing one of these names and meditating on it bring you closer to Jesus this Advent?

"The Lord Is Salvation"

Read aloud or summarize:

When the angel appeared first to Mary and then to Joseph, telling them about the impending birth of a child, the message of what they were to name the child was the same: "You shall call His name Jesus, for He will save His people from their sins" (Matthew 1:21 NASB; see also Luke 1:31). Throughout the Bible we see that names hold great meaning and often are used to describe that a significant change has come or is coming. This is certainly true in the Christmas story.

In *The Wonder of Christmas* (pp. 50-51), Ed Robb points out a connection between Jesus' name and that of Joshua, one of the heroes of the Old Testament. What is the connection? *Jesus* is the Greek form of the Hebrew name *Joshua.*[2]

We learn of Joshua's story in the Book of Numbers, in which we find the Israelites living in the desert. After being freed from Egypt's tyrannical slavery, they lived for a time in the wilderness, and now they have made it to the edge of the promised land of Canaan.

In Numbers 13, God tells Moses, their leader, to send some scouts into Canaan to check out the scene and observe the people who are living there. Ten of the spies come back with a report.

Discuss:

- Read aloud Numbers 13:27-28, 32. What did these ten scouts conclude?
- Now read aloud Numbers 14:7-9. What was the perspective of the other two scouts, Joshua and Caleb?

Read aloud or summarize:

Before sending the spies to explore the land, Moses changed Hoshea's name to Joshua (see Numbers 13:16). In doing so, Moses wove together two names—Jehovah (*Yahweh*), the proper name of the God of Israel,[3] and Hoshea, which means "salvation."[4] This formed a new name, Joshua (*Yehoshua* in Hebrew), meaning "the Lord is salvation,"[5] or God saves.

Why change Joshua's name from "salvation" to "the Lord is salvation"? The distinction is not immediately clear until we discover how the scouting trip turned out. As we've just heard, ten of the scouts came back and reported there was no way the Israelites could defeat the Canaanites living there and claim their God-given land. But two of the scouts, Caleb and Joshua, believed that the Lord would be victorious. Caleb and Joshua saw the same obstacles as the other scouts, but they were looking not to their own ability for salvation but to God's ability to do what God had promised.

Discuss:

- Read aloud Joshua 1:1-5. How did Joshua's story ultimately turn out?
- What mental shift happens between "salvation" and "the Lord is salvation"? Can you describe a time in your life when you experienced this shift in thinking? What happened?
- The name *Jesus*, which is the Greek form of *Joshua*, meaning "the Lord is salvation," would have had great meaning to Mary and Joseph. What does learning about this connection between Jesus and Joshua help you to better understand about Jesus?
- Read aloud Ephesians 2:8. How does the knowledge of God's gift of salvation in Jesus change your perspective during this season of Advent?

The Name that Saves

Read aloud or summarize:

The angel declared, "You shall call His name Jesus, for He will save His people from their sins" (Matthew 1:21 NASB). There's no question about it—sin is a big problem in our world. Often it feels as if the state of the world is beyond repair. A quick scan of today's headlines confirms this. Humanity is broken. We don't have the ability or power to save ourselves. God knew that we desperately need a Savior, so God sent Jesus.

Discuss:

- In the simplest terms, *sin* is rejection of God. But we don't use the word *sin* very often in our daily conversations. Why do you think that is? What are some other words we use for *sin*? (e.g., *pride, temptation, tendencies, human nature, mistakes*)
- Scripture says that Jesus will save "His people" from their sins. Today many people debate who "His people" are, but the Bible makes it clear. According to Romans 10:9, who are "His people"?

A New Name

Note: This might be an emotional activity for some in your group. Be sensitive to and aware of anyone in the group who might not want to share his or her response.

Discuss:

- Have you ever wanted to choose a new name for yourself? If so, what would you have chosen and why?

Read aloud or summarize:

Throughout the Bible, we read of God changing people's names to signify a new meaning or purpose for them. In Genesis we read that God changed the name of Abram, which means "exalted father,"[6] to Abraham, which means "father of a multitude,"[7] as a sign of God's promise that Abraham would become the father of many nations (Genesis 17:5). Imagine how Abraham, who was already ninety-nine years old and had no children at the time God changed his name to "father of many nations," must have felt to hear a promise that seemed virtually impossible.

Likewise, in the New Testament, we read of Jesus changing Simon's name to Peter, the Greek word for *rock*,[8] so that Peter would forever be reminded that he was to be the foundation of the church (Matthew 16:18). The road Peter walked as a disciple of Jesus was certainly bumpy, and there were times he doubted his own faith and purpose; but he continued to follow and spread the word about the Savior.

Though both Abraham and Peter faltered and sometimes doubted God's promises to them, they could always look back and remember the names God had given them and be reassured of God's power and presence in their lives.

Activity:

- Distribute two index cards or slips of paper to each group member.

- *Say:* The world is quick to give us many names. Often these labels are given in judgment and are intended to shame us or keep us stuck in the past. Sometimes we give these names to ourselves, which makes them hard to shake. On one of the cards/papers you've been given, write a name or label that you have been living under. You will not have to share this name with anyone, so allow yourself to be honest in your answer.

- After a moment, distribute copies of the scriptures on page 34. (Prepare in advance. If you are not making photocopies, it might be helpful to use bold text for the names God gives in these verses.)

- *Say:* The wonderful news about Christmas is that if you accept God's gift of love and salvation in Jesus, then God wholeheartedly and joyfully gives you a new name. God's promises aren't empty promises. If God promises something, God will be faithful to fulfill it. That's what God did through Jesus. God promised to come for you, and it happened. God has pursued you through the heavens and the earth. Take a few minutes now to read through the verses on this sheet. As you read, allow God to speak these names over you. On the second card/paper you were given earlier, write one name from Scripture that you hear God speaking over you today.

- When everyone is finished, encourage group members to rip up the cards that contain their old names or labels. Then go around the room and ask for volunteers to share the new names God spoke over them today. Suggest they post their new names somewhere they will see them often to remind themselves of God's promises for their lives.

The one who is the true light, who gives light to everyone, was coming into the world. He came into the very world he created, but the world didn't recognize him. He came to his own people, and even they rejected him. But to all who believed him and accepted him, he gave the right to become **children** *of God. They are reborn—not with a physical birth resulting from human passion or plan, but a birth that comes from God.*

(John 1:9-13 NLT)

Therefore, there is now no condemnation for those who are in Christ Jesus, because through Christ Jesus the law of the Spirit who gives life has set you **free** *from the law of sin and death.*

(Romans 8:1-2)

"I have called you by name; you are **mine.***"*

(Isaiah 43:1 CEB)

"I will be a Father to you, / and you will be my **sons and daughters***, / says the Lord Almighty."*

(2 Corinthians 6:18)

"I no longer call you servants, because a servant does not know his master's business. Instead, I have called you **friends***, for everything that I learned from my Father I have made known to you."*

(John 15:15)

For we are God's **masterpiece***. He has created us anew in Christ Jesus, so we can do the good things he planned for us long ago.*

(Ephesians 2:10 NLT)

See how very much our Father loves us, for he calls us his **children***, and that is what we are!*

(1 John 3:1 NLT)

Discuss:

- How does our new name change the way we walk on this earth—the way we live with and love others?

Closing (10 minutes)

Lighting the Advent Wreath

Present the Advent wreath and prepare to light the first and second candles. You might dim the lights or play some soft background music during this time, possibly some traditional Christmas hymns such as "Silent Night" and "I Heard the Bells on Christmas Day."

Read aloud or summarize:

This week, the second week of Advent, we light the candle of Peace and reflect on the wonder of the precious name of Jesus, our Prince of Peace. Isaiah 9:6 proclaims, "A child is born to us, a son is given to us, / and authority will be on his shoulders. / He will be named / Wonderful Counselor, Mighty God, / Eternal Father, Prince of Peace" (CEB).

- Spend about five minutes in silence together, prompting the group to ask God to help us claim the names given us as God's children and identify specific ways we can hold on to those promises. If you choose, invite participants to journal during this time.

Watching for Wonder Challenge

Encourage participants to be watching for the names of Jesus as they read God's Word, listen to Christmas music, and go about their daily activities during this Christmas season. Ask them to meditate throughout the week—and the entire season of Advent—on the particular name of Jesus that they chose during today's session, inviting Jesus to draw them closer to him and increase their sense of wonder of who he is and what he has done. Invite them to journal about what they see or share their thoughts with a family member or friend.

Closing Prayer

Dear Lord, we praise your name today, giving you thanks for being our Savior, our Counselor, our Mighty God, our Prince of Peace. You are our Teacher, Friend, and Father. Thank you for sending Jesus so that we can know you and experience the richness of your grace and love. Help us to walk in your light this week. In Jesus' name. Amen.

Additional Material

Different Points of View, Same God

Read aloud or summarize:

The Gospel writers tell the same story in different ways, drawing on their own personalities and approaches to life. For this reason, there are differences among the four Gospels. The Gospels of Mark and John, for example, do not say one word about the birth of Jesus. Instead, Mark focuses on Jesus' ministry, and John focuses on Jesus' theology. Matthew and Luke both tell the story of the nativity, but each tells it his own way. Matthew's account is more precise and factual, especially when it comes to details about Jesus' heritage—which makes sense when you consider Matthew was part of the Jewish establishment. Luke's retelling is more like a story, emphasizing how Jesus came as savior to both Jews and Gentiles—which also makes sense because Luke was a Gentile.

For the sake of comparison, let's take a look at one story about Jesus that appears in each of the four Gospels—the feeding of the five thousand.

Activity:

- Divide into four groups and have each group read one of the following Gospel accounts:
  o Matthew 14:14-21
  o Mark 6:35-44

- o Luke 9:10-17
- o John 6:1-13
- Have each group note the following:
  - o What four or five words or phrases stand out to you in this passage?
  - o What message do you think the Gospel writer wanted to give by telling this story?
  - o What does each account have to say about the name of Jesus?
- Come back together and have the groups share their answers.

Discuss:

- Why do you think each of the four Gospels tells about Jesus in these different ways?
- Though they were very different men with different perspectives, the Gospel writers were all committed to telling the message of Christ. What point of view do you carry that affects your view of Jesus? How have you allowed that point of view to unite or separate you from other believers?

Signs from God

Read aloud or summarize:

When the angel of the Lord appeared to Joseph, he spoke the exact words the prophet Isaiah had spoken long before: "Therefore the Lord Himself will give you a sign: Behold, a virgin will be with child and bear a son, and she will call His name Immanuel" (Isaiah 7:14 NASB).

Mary and Joseph were probably familiar with Isaiah's prophecy. Maybe they had heard those words their whole lives, but how do you think they must have felt to hear them from the mouth of an angel? Were they elated to be part of the prophecy or terrified? Was the mention of Immanuel enough to quiet all their doubts and assure them that what was happening was indeed from God?

Discuss:

- The Bible is full of stories of God speaking to his people through extraordinary measures such as angels and burning bushes. Many of us learned these stories when we were children—Jonah and the big fish, Balaam's talking donkey, Moses and the burning bush, Jesus feeding the five thousand, Daniel in the lion's den, and many others. What is/was your favorite Bible story and how did it shape your view of God?
- Have you ever experienced what you believe was a sign from God? If so, what were the circumstances?

Read aloud or summarize:

Though we have not received angelic proclamations as Mary and Joseph did, we, too, have access to the promises of God in God's Word; and we are blessed to know that God's ultimate promise has been fulfilled in Jesus—Immanuel, God with us. We also have the Holy Spirit—the perfect Counselor and Coach—to guide and comfort us through whatever life may bring our way.

Discuss:

- Read aloud John 14:25-27 and discuss the following:
  - o What promise of guidance did Jesus give the disciples?
  - o Why do we not have to rely on visible signs today? How has God given us everything we need to hear and follow God? (We have the Word of God at our fingertips, the example of Christ, and the Holy Spirit within us, speaking words of life to us.)

Session 3

The Wonder of a Manger

Planning the Session

Session Goals

Participants will be encouraged to:

- Consider what Jesus' humble birth tells us about his leadership.
- Discover that although Jesus came to rescue all of humanity, he came just for each one of us too.
- Explore the ways Jesus taught us how to live as his disciples, loving and serving one another.

Materials Needed

- *The Wonder of Christmas* book (one for every participant)
- Bibles (extras for participants)
- *The Wonder of Christmas DVD*, DVD player

- Markerboard or chart paper, markers
- Advent wreath, candles, matches

Optional:

- Writing paper or journals, pens or pencils for journaling (provide or have participants bring their own)
- Recordings of Christmas carols or hymns

Preparation

- Read and reflect on Chapter 3, "The Wonder of a Manger."
- Read through the session outline and select the material you plan to cover.
- Read and reflect on the following scriptures:
  - o Zephaniah 3:17
  - o Luke 15
  - o Luke 2:4-12
  - o John 8:1-11
  - o Colossians 1:19-20
  - o Philippians 2:5-7
- Prepare the room and gather the necessary materials. Cue the video for Session 3. Be sure to set out an Advent wreath to light during the closing. (Don't forget matches!) You may want to play some soft Christmas music during this time. If you choose, you may have participants journal during this time.

Getting Started (10 minutes)

Opening Activity

Welcome participants as they arrive.

Read aloud or summarize:

When we have an experience that forever changes our perspective, we sometimes say that it was a "burning bush moment"—which is a reference to the story of Moses in Exodus 3. One ordinary day Moses went to tend his sheep and God met him in the wilderness, appearing in the form of a bush that was on fire but did not burn up. Through that experience, Moses received a call from God that changed his life. One day life was normal; the next the world as he knew it was turned upside down.

Today we are going to talk about how the manger represents a perspective-changing "burning bush moment" for all of humanity.

Discuss:

- Have you ever experienced a life-changing "burning bush" moment in your life? What happened?
- Are there any movies, books, or trips that have completely changed your perspective on someone or something?

Opening Prayer

Lord, open our hearts and minds to hear a word from you. Help us to experience you in a new way as we think about the wonder of you coming to earth to turn the world upside down, save us, and show us how to serve one another. In Jesus' holy name. Amen.

Content Review and Application (40 minutes)

Note: This section allows approximately 10–12 minutes for a video segment and 25–28 minutes for discussion. More content has been provided than you will have time to cover. Select in advance those questions you would like to discuss, putting a check mark beside each one.

Video

Play Session 3 (running time 11:41).

Discuss:

- Why do you think God's Son was allowed by God to be born in a lowly manger?
- How is the manger a harbinger of Christ's entire ministry and mission? What does it teach us?

- How can the manger help to awaken us to the wonder of Christmas?

Study and Discussion (25–28 minutes)

Humble Beginnings

Read aloud or summarize:

The Christmas carol "Away in a Manger" creates a serene, peaceful picture of baby Jesus sleeping on the hay in a manger because there was no room in the inn (see Luke 2:7). But when we step back and take another look at the words in this familiar carol, it's odd to picture the Son of God lying in a barn surrounded by farm animals. This doesn't seem the best place for a newborn baby, let alone *this baby*— the Christ Child, God's own Son sent from above, the Savior of the world. Certainly God could have orchestrated much more appropriate circumstances!

But there was something important and intentional about this setting. Ed Robb writes, "The manger was a harbinger of Christ's entire ministry. It spoke volumes about the way the Sovereign Ruler of the universe intended to win back lost children—not by overwhelming us with might, but winning us with love" (p. 74). God could have made Jesus' birth a national or world event, but that was not God's plan. By design, God wanted to set the stage of Jesus' reign from the start.

Discuss:

- Read Luke 2:4-12. What does this scene tell you about the picture God wanted to paint of Jesus' coming ministry?

Activity:

The manger was just the beginning of Jesus showing us a new way to live. Read about Jesus' encounter with a woman brought before him in John 8:1-11. On a markerboard or chart paper, make two columns, one titled "Leaders" and another "Jesus." After reading the passage aloud, brainstorm and list in the Leaders column three or four words you would use to describe how the Pharisees (the religious leaders of the day) handled the situation. In the Jesus column, list words to describe how Jesus handled the situation. Discuss the differences and what this teaches us about how Jesus wants us to lead others.

Discuss:

- Read Psalm 145:8-9. How can or does this description of Jesus affect your view of his leadership in your life?

The Great Pursuit

Read aloud or summarize:

Luke's Gospel says, "For the Son of Man came to seek and to save the lost" (19:10). Throughout the centuries, God told his people again and again that they would be rescued, that they had not been forgotten, and that God's covenant with them would be kept. So, when the time was right, God sent Jesus, whose birth was part of a direct mission to save God's people.

Have you ever lost something dear to you? If so, chances are you did whatever you could to find the lost object. Why? Because when something is precious to you, you're willing to go to great lengths to get it back. And that is what God did for us by sending Jesus.

Many classic children's books revolve around the idea of searching for something that has been lost. The story of loss and desire is universal to us all. In Luke 15, Jesus tells three parables to describe God's unfailing love for and pursuit of his lost people. In order to get a different perspective on these parables, which may be very familiar, listen to these parables of Jesus as told in a children's Bible.

Activity:

- Read aloud the following parables from a children's Bible:
  o The Lost Sheep (Luke 15:1-7)
  o The Lost Coin (Luke 15:8-10)
  o The Lost Son (Luke 15:11-32)
- How does hearing these stories from a different perspective change the way you hear and understand these parables?

- Now read aloud Colossians 1:19-20. As Sally Lloyd Jones describes so beautifully in *The Jesus Storybook Bible*, "You see, no matter what, in spite of everything, God would love his children—with a Never Stopping, Never Giving Up, Unbreaking, Always and Forever Love."[9] God was intentionally pursuing us, God's children, and the manger is a beautiful picture of the lengths God was willing to go in order to reach us, whatever the cost.
- How can the knowledge of God's "all in" pursuit of us affect the way we live our everyday lives?

God Goes Big, for You

Read aloud or summarize:

The beautiful nativity scenes in our homes and churches are meant to inspire us during the Advent season. We can look upon the calm, beautiful scene and visualize what that first Christmas might have looked like. It's a nice idea, but when we consider the facts given in the Bible, we quickly realize there was nothing romantic about Jesus' birth. Here were Mary and Joseph, who were alone, going through this messy, momentous event in a barn full of hay and animals.

Jesus' birth was revolutionary for all of humanity, but Scripture tells us clearly that God pursues each and every child with just as much intensity. So we can imagine that at the same time God was revolutionizing the world through Christ's humble birth, God was working in the lives of both Mary and Joseph, using this shared experience to bind and knit them together as husband and wife.

Discuss:

- Have you ever been through an experience with someone that bonded you together in a way you never would have expected?
- In the midst of the big picture of what God is doing in the world, is it hard for you to believe that God intensely cares about you? Have volunteers read aloud Luke 12:6-7, 1 Peter 5:7, Zephaniah 3:17, and Luke 15:4-7. What do these verses say about God's pursuit of each of us? How is the

wonder of what God did for us through the manger both big and small, physical and spiritual?

- How would you describe what the wonder of the manger means for you personally?

How to Be Human

Read aloud or summarize:

Jesus came to earth, through the wonder of a humble manger so that we could live eternally with God. He lived among us so that we could watch and learn from him how to be truly free by living through the power of God with the Holy Spirit guiding us.

Jesus came to be a servant, a point he made repeatedly. Why did he feel the need to emphasize this point? Perhaps because he knew that having the attitude of a servant would be hard for us. He knew how we would struggle with greed and comparison. He knew that, left to our own devices, we would give in to self-protection and our need to define "us" and "them." Jesus responded to all these desires by demonstrating and teaching about servanthood.

Discuss:

- Read the following scriptures and identify the traits of servanthood exhibited by Jesus in each scenario: Philippians 2:5-7; John 4:7-10; Matthew 9:11-13.
- Read Luke 10:25-37, the parable of the Good Samaritan. *Ask*: Who are your neighbors? How might the Lord be leading you, this group, or your church to meet the needs of your community? What support or help do you need? What might this group's role be in modeling Jesus' attitude of servanthood to our neighbors during this Advent season and beyond?

Closing (10 minutes)

Lighting the Advent Wreath

Present the Advent wreath and prepare to light the first, second, and third candles. You might dim the lights or play some soft background music during this time, possibly some traditional Christmas hymns such as "Away in a Manger" and "It Came Upon a Midnight Clear."

Read aloud or summarize:

This week, the third week of Advent, we light the Love candle and reflect on the wonder of the manger, which represents God's rescue mission to come and save us as beloved children.

- Spend a few minutes in silence together, prompting the group to pray that God would help us to believe in and experience the extraordinary, never-ceasing love God has for us, and to ask for ways that we can share this wonderful love with others this season and beyond. If you choose, invite participants to journal during this time.

Watching for Wonder Challenge

Encourage participants to be watching with new eyes for evidence of God's sacrificial, saving love and to find a way to share the love of Christ by serving others this week. Invite them to journal about what they see or experience or to share their thoughts with a family member or friend.

Closing Prayer

Abba Father, today we stand in wonder at the sight of the manger, a symbol of your great pursuit of us. Help us walk in your love every day, remembering what you did for us and how you have shown your love by never abandoning us. Imprint that love deeply on our hearts so that we can extend it to others. Thank you for sending your Son, Jesus, to model how to walk and live on this earth with all your children, whom you love equally. In Jesus' name. Amen.

Additional Material

God in the Messy Places

Read aloud or summarize:

If it were up to us, our lives would be free of complications. In fact, we typically orchestrate our lives so that any type of inconvenience is minimized or eliminated altogether. But every good story contains conflict, including the biblical Christmas story. Often it is the complications that arise in a story that make it worth reading; they make us want to learn more.

When writers craft stories, they purposefully complicate a character's situation by creating obstacles in order to move the story along. For example, a writer might begin telling the story of a family that has set out on a cross-county road trip, and then their car breaks down in the middle of nowhere. Now the situation is complicated and begs for the story to be told. Let's have some fun with this idea of complicating a story.

- Have members break into pairs or small groups and brainstorm two or three complications for the following situations (or situations of their own choosing).
  - A group of siblings plan a party for their parents' 50th wedding anniversary.
  - A teacher plans a class field trip to the zoo.
  - A woman or man comes home to discover a package on the front door step.
  - A young person goes on a reality TV show.
- After allowing about five minutes, come back together and share ideas.

Read aloud or summarize:

Oftentimes it is in the complications—when we are pushed and shoved and thrust out of our comfort zones—that God shows up in a big way.

Think about Mary and Joseph being told to travel back to Bethlehem for the census. We think waiting in line at the airport is torture; just imagine traveling approximately eighty miles on foot or the back of an animal while pregnant! But in the midst of the unlikely and the inconvenient, God had a plan.

- Read Micah 5:2. What was God's plan for Jesus' birth—long before he was born?
- When we are faced with inconvenient circumstances or unexpected disruptions in our plans, it can be easy to become frustrated and angry at life's circumstances. But in those places, we can know that God is present and working. Read Romans 8:28. Could it be that God wants to use even the inconvenient, unlikely, and uncomfortable places in our lives to draw us closer? How does God use the "complication" of the unlikely crib of a manger to awaken us to the wonder of Christmas?

Hidden in Plain Sight
Read aloud or summarize:

Have you ever witnessed a young child playing hide and seek with a parent? The game always ends the same way, doesn't it? The child finds the parent. Why? Because the parent hides in order to be found so that the child will experience the joy of discovery.

The manger tells us that Jesus came to earth because God wants to be found by us—in fact, God guarantees it.

- Have you ever felt that God was hiding from you or was difficult to "find"? Read Jeremiah 29:11-14. What does God promise us in these verses?
- Jesus delivered on all these promises. Through him, through the little baby in a humble manger, God revealed himself fully to us and gave eternal life to those who have believed. Read John 6:29. Do you ever have doubts about God or Jesus? How does this verse speak to those doubts? Who does this scripture specifically say is responsible for faith? How does this verse challenge your ideas about faith and a relationship with God?

Session 4

The Wonder of a Promise

Planning the Session

Session Goals

Participants will be encouraged to:

- Consider the ways that Jesus fulfills the promises of God.
- Think about the ways they can keep the promise of Christmas by loving and serving others.

Materials Needed

- *The Wonder of Christmas* book (one for every participant)
- Bibles (extras for participants)
- *The Wonder of Christmas DVD*, DVD player

- Markerboard or chart paper, markers
- Advent wreath, candles, matches

Optional:
- Writing paper or journals, pens or pencils for journaling (provide or have participants bring their own)
- Recordings of Christmas carols or hymns
- Copies of scriptures on page 62 (one for each participant)

Preparation

- Read and reflect on Chapter 4, "The Wonder of a Promise."
- Read through the session outline and select the material you plan to cover.
- Read and reflect on the following Scriptures:
  o Matthew 1:22-23
  o Ezekiel 37:27-28
  o Acts 17:25
  o 2 Corinthians 8:9
  o 2 Peter 1:3
  o John 15:5
- Prepare the room and gather the necessary materials. Cue the video for Session 4. Be sure to set out an Advent wreath to light during the closing. (Don't forget matches!) You may want to play some soft Christmas music during this time. If you choose, you may have participants journal during this time.
- *Optional:* For your last meeting, you might want to celebrate your study and the season by having a party or potluck. If you like, invite group members to help with planning and divide up responsibilities.

Getting Started (10 minutes)

Opening Activity

Welcome participants as they arrive.

Read aloud or summarize:

It's virtually impossible to make it through the Christmas season without encountering some adaptation of Charles Dickens's classic novella *A Christmas Carol*. Which movie version of *A Christmas Carol* is your favorite and why? (Pause for responses.)

Christmas tales like *A Christmas Carol* often involve transformation. Just as the character of Scrooge is transformed, we are transformed by the promise of Christmas; and we are called to pass that promise on to others. This will be our focus as we conclude our study today.

Opening Prayer

Heavenly Father, thank you for the opportunity to gather and remember the extraordinary promises that are ours to claim through the events of that first Christmas long ago. Open our eyes and ears to hear you speaking to us today. Guide us in your truth. In Jesus' name. Amen.

Content Review and Application (40 minutes)

Note: This section allows approximately 10–12 minutes for a video segment and 25–28 minutes for discussion. More content has been provided than you will have time to cover. Select in advance those questions you would like to discuss, putting a check mark beside each one.

Video

Play Session 4 (running time 11:32).

Discuss:

- What is the promise of Christmas, and what does this promise mean to you personally?
- How would your life be different if you truly lived the promise of Christmas every day, remembering that God is always with you?
- How can you share this promise with others? What does it mean to be the presence of Christ with other people?

Study and Discussion (25–28 minutes)

God with Us

Read aloud or summarize:

The promise of Christmas transforms our view of God. The people of Israel knew much about their God. As Rob Renfroe points out, the Israelites who lived before Jesus thought of God in three ways—God *above us*, God *against us*, and God *for us*. First, they clearly understood the idea of God *above us*. They worshiped and acknowledged God as the Creator of everything and as the One who led them. Second, as they acknowledged God's power and authority when they sinned, they believed in God *against us*. And third, when they thought they were doing everything just right, therefore deserving God's favor, they were able to believe in God *for us*.

Discuss:

- How do you think most people view God—*above us, against us,* or *for us*? Explain your response.
- Has there been a time when you identified with one of these descriptions of God?

Read aloud or summarize:

It's tempting to try to put God into one of these categories, but God wants us to have another understanding. This is why, on that first Christmas Day, God turned the tables on all of our preconceived notions about who God is and what God can do. God's desire is not to be God *above us* or God *against us* or even God *for us*. God wants to be God *with us*.

Discuss:

- Read Matthew 1:22-23. In this passage the angel quotes Isaiah 7:14, which foretold Jesus' birth. What do you imagine the Old Testament Israelites thought about the prophecy of God *with us*?

Read aloud or summarize:

The Israelites had experienced a long history with God, but they did not believe that anyone could attain an intimate relationship with God. They thought that someone had to intercede for them—a prophet, leader, priest, or king. But God had made a promise to be with God's people always, and God meant to fulfill that promise in a bigger way than they could have imagined—Immanuel, God *with us.*

Discuss:

- Read Ezekiel 37:27-28. How does God *with us*—as opposed to God *above us, against us,* or *for us*—transform your idea of who God is and what he can do in your life?

The Body of Christ
Read aloud or summarize:

The promise of Christmas—Immanuel, God with us—is a gift for not only those of us who believe; it also is a gift that we are called to pass on to others. As the church, the body of Christ, we are called to go where Jesus went and to care for people the way Jesus did—to truly be *with* them. One of the reasons that Jesus came to earth and inhabited a physical body was so that we would know how to respond to others.

Activity:

- On a markerboard or chart paper, draw a simple outline of the human body (stick figures are fine).
- Label the corresponding body parts with the following Scriptures that describe Jesus in action:
    o Head – John 3:1-16
    o Hair – Luke 7:36-48
    o Hands – Mark 5:25-34
    o Legs – Mark 2:1-12
    o Feet – John 13:1-17

- Assign the body parts and corresponding Scriptures to pairs or small groups. Ask them to read the passage together and then answer the following questions:
  - o Why does this scripture correspond with the body part given?
  - o In one or two words, how would you describe Jesus' actions and/or response to those he encountered in this passage?
  - o (*For example:* John 3:1-16 corresponds to the head because Nicodemus was searching for answers to his questions. One or two words to describe Jesus in this scene might be *patient* or *not threatened.*)
- Come back together and ask each group or pair to share their responses. Write the descriptive words next to the figure you've drawn on the markerboard or chart paper.
- *Ask:* How do these descriptive words inspire you to live as Jesus lived? Where or how is he asking you to use your physical gifts to serve others?

The Abundance of the Promise

Read aloud or summarize:

As we strive to focus on Jesus during Advent, it's easy to be distracted by the mantra of consumerism: *the more, the better.* Indulging in the food and festivities of the season can be harmless enough—after all, it *is* a celebration. But our culture seems to have adopted this mantra year-round. We are bombarded daily with messages that tell us we need more of this or that in order to live a happy life. Many of us have come to believe the myth of scarcity—the idea that we do not have enough of what we need.

Discuss:

- How and when have you found yourself influenced by advertising or other messages promoting the idea of *more*? How did these message affect your view of your life?

Read aloud or summarize:

We all buy into the myth of scarcity in different areas of our lives, whether we feel there is never enough time, money, resources, or possessions. And when we buy into this myth, we close our hands tightly around what we already have, falling into greed and self-protection. (Remember Scrooge?)

When these feelings creep in during Advent, we need to turn our eyes to the wonder of Christmas—to the reminder that Jesus came to earth to remind us of his abundant love and limitless resources.

Discuss:

- Read 2 Corinthians 8:9 and 2 Peter 1:3. What do these verses have to say about what we have been given through Christ? How has he equipped us?
- Acts 17:25 says God is "not served by human hands, as if he needed anything. Rather, he himself gives everyone life and breath and everything else" (NIV). God doesn't *need* us to serve. So why does God ask us to do it? (Hint: When we serve, we are reminded that God put us first and that God is our Provider, so we don't have to worry about running out of what we have to give. When we serve, we are reminded of God's great love for us, which leads us to worship God by loving and serving others.)

Keeping Christmas

Read aloud or summarize:

Christmas is the story of a star shining bright, of a name declared in joy, of a manger humbly waiting, and a promise given freely. It is the story of what happened on a bright, starlit night some two thousand years ago in the village of Bethlehem; but it's also the story of what's happening right now, right where you are.

We keep the promise of Christmas when we tell a lost, scared, and angry world about the gospel of Jesus. Just as Jesus modeled, we learn

55

that in order to reach others we must be *with* them. How do we do that? Rob Renfroe suggests three ways:

- We must understand the people we want to reach.
- We must remember our own stories.
- We must care about others' stories.

Discuss:

- Which of these three ways comes easiest to you? Which is most difficult?

Read aloud or summarize:

Throughout the Old Testament, we read about the Lord commanding his people to dedicate the *firstfruits* of their crops, their livestock, and even their children to God. *First* suggests things that are given priority. *Fruits* are the products we see on the tree or plant that produced them; the fruit develops as a result of being connected to the branch or vine. In John 15:5, Jesus says, "If you remain in me and I in you, you will bear much fruit; apart from me you can do nothing."

Discuss:

- What does it mean to say that the Lord wants the firstfruits of our lives? What does this have to do with how God wants us to love and serve others? (*Hint:* When we live out of our own resources, we are tempted to look out for our own needs first and give out of our excess. But when we live connected to Christ and draw from his resources, we are willing to give first, putting others before ourselves.)
- It has been said that vague commitments often produce vague results, while specific commitments lead to progress and growth. Do you think this is true? If so, how have you experienced this is your own life?
- What are some practical ways you can "keep" the promise of Christmas this season—making the promise real in the lives of others by being the presence of God to those who are confused, hurting, or lost?

Closing (10 minutes)

Lighting the Advent Wreath

Present the Advent wreath and prepare to light all four candles. You might dim the lights or play some soft background music during this time, possibly some traditional Christmas hymns such as "Come, Thou Long-Expected Jesus."

Read aloud or summarize:

This week, the fourth week of Advent, we light the Joy candle and reflect on the wonder of the promise that is Jesus. We thank God that all of God's promises to us are fulfilled in the birth, life, and death of Jesus, and we rejoice in God's faithfulness in loving us.

- Spend a few minutes in silence together, prompting the group to pray that God would show us ways to keep the promise of Christmas—to make it real in others' lives—by being God's hands and feet in the lives of others. If you choose, invite participants to journal during this time.

Watching for Wonder Challenge

Encourage participants to be watching for ways they can "keep" the promise of Christmas not only this season but also in the coming year. Invite them to be the presence of God in the lives of others—loving, serving, and blessing others in the name of Jesus. Remind them to journal about what they see or experience, or to share theirs thoughts with a family member or friend.

Closing Prayer

Our loving and faithful God, we thank you for all the amazing promises you have given us, and we praise you for fulfilling the ultimate promise through Jesus Christ—Immanuel, God with us. Thank you for this precious gift, Lord, and help us to remember all that we have learned during this study, keeping your promise throughout the year. We praise you, Lord, for the gift of this time together to study your Word. In Jesus' name. Amen.

Additional Material

Great Expectations

Read aloud or summarize:

Many of us enjoy watching Christmas movies, and some of the funniest ones are those that feature full-blown Christmas disasters. You know the kind—someone wants to have the "perfect Christmas," and along comes a multitude of disastrous events that leave everything in hilarious shambles.

Discuss:

- What are the plotlines of some of your favorite Christmas comedies? In these movies, what do the characters start out wanting from the upcoming Christmas season?
- We laugh because these movies are hilarious and outrageous, but also because we see the truth in them. We understand the characters' over-the-top desire to make the Christmas season meaningful because the weight of our own expectations for the season can be heavy, even crushing. When have you had this experience, and what expectations did you bring to the season? What was the result?

Read aloud or summarize:

We decorate, shop, plan, cook, clean, and party in a quest for meaning and connection during the busy season. But too often we end up disappointed despite all our hard work. Why? Because we want something from the season that it cannot give. We want something from our families, friends, bank accounts, and churches that they cannot give—because what our hearts desire is simply more of Jesus.

We want God, plain and simple. We long for God's presence, but often we mistake this longing as a desire for things that we can see and taste and touch. We put our hope in things other than God, which causes us to sin.

But the miracle of Christmas is that Jesus comes to be with us, turning our faces away from our empty desires and toward him.

Discuss:

- Read aloud Matthew 11:28, Mark 2:17, and Luke 19:10. How does Jesus respond to our desire—and our disappointment—in the Christmas season?

Just the Facts, Please

Read aloud or summarize:

We live by facts. We know that the sun will set at night and rise again in the morning. We know that the weather and seasons will change. We know that things will be born and things will die. We are trained to operate according to what has already happened, what is certain, what is measureable, and what is definable.

Discuss:

- What are some facts you live by? (*For example:* "I leave the house every morning at 7:00 a.m." or "We go camping every summer.")

Read aloud or summarize:

For some of us, living by facts makes the concept of faith hard to process and embrace. We desperately want to feel Jesus' presence in our lives; we want to live daily in his strength and grace and love. But too often that feels difficult when we can't see him or touch him or hear his audible words. We don't expect a surprise visit from an angel, sharing a word from God.

In Luke 1:26-38, we read about the angel visiting Mary to tell her that she would become pregnant and give birth to Jesus. Scripture does not tell us many facts about Mary, but what we know is that God entrusted this seemingly ordinary girl with an extraordinary promise—a promise that would change not only her life but also the whole world.

How must she have felt after that supernatural announcement? According to Scripture, Mary immediately responded by saying that she believed what the angel said was true. But how might Mary have felt when the angel left and she was all alone to process this news? She likely did not *feel* pregnant in that moment. There were no tests she could take to confirm what the angel had said was true. There was no immediate change in her body. She had been given a promise, but she had to wait for God's timing to experience the fulfillment of it.

Discuss:

- What are some things that we do by faith, trusting that "the promise" will come to fruition one day? (*For example:* planting seeds in the garden, expecting that one day they will grow into flowers.)
- Have you, like Mary, ever received a promise that required you to wait for its fulfillment? How did you respond, and how did your response affect you?

Read aloud or summarize:

Because we often live by facts, expecting immediate gratification, it can be difficult for us to live by faith. Most of the time we hope for the best and wonder, *Can God hear me? Is God speaking to me? Is God really with me now?*

All promises from God come true. In God, promises come to fruition. And there is no promise more wondrous or real than the promise of Christmas—of Immanuel, God with us; God come to save God's people. Christ was the Old Testament prophecy come true, and he is just as active and attentive in our lives today through the Holy Spirit.

Activity:

- Distribute copies of the scriptures on page 62 that tell of God's promise to be with us always. (Prepare in advance.)
- Allow several minutes for participants to read the scriptures silently and meditate on them. Ask participants to think about one way in which they need God's presence—or to be reassured of God's presence—today. Ask if anyone is willing to share his or her thoughts or prayers with the group.
- *Ask:* How does the promise of Christmas—that Jesus is Immanuel, God *with us* today, tomorrow, and forever—give you hope and peace for your life right now?

Jesus Christ is the same yesterday and today and forever.

(*Hebrews 13:8 NIV*)

"*For I know the plans I have for you,*" declares the Lord, "*plans to prosper you and not to harm you, plans to give you hope and a future.*"

(*Jeremiah 29:11 NIV*)

I'm convinced that nothing can separate us from God's love in Christ Jesus our Lord: not death or life, not angels or rulers, not present things or future things, not powers or height or depth, or any other thing that is created.

(*Romans 8:38-39 CEB*)

[*Jesus said,*] "*All this I have spoken while still with you. But the Advocate, the Holy Spirit, whom the Father will send in my name, will teach you all things and will remind you of everything I have said to you. Peace I leave with you; my peace I give you. I do not give to you as the world gives. Do not let your hearts be troubled and do not be afraid.*"

(*John 14:25-27 NIV*)

"*Are you tired? Worn out? Burned out on religion? Come to me. Get away with me and you'll recover your life. I'll show you how to take a real rest. Walk with me and work with me—watch how I do it. Learn the unforced rhythms of grace. I won't lay anything heavy or ill-fitting on you. Keep company with me and you'll learn to live freely and lightly.*"

(*Matthew 11:28-29* The Message)

Notes

1   Saint Augustine of Hippo, *The Confessions of Saint Augustine* (Stillwell, KS: Digireads.com Publishing, 2005), 25.

2   *Strong's Concordance Online*, s.v. "Iésous," accessed June 3, 2016, http://biblehub.com/greek/2424.htm.

3   *Strong's Concordance Online*, s.v. "Yhvh" (Jehovah), accessed June 3, 2016, http://biblehub.com/hebrew/3068.htm.

4   *Strong's Concordance Online*, s.v. "Hoshea," accessed June 3, 2016, http://biblehub.com/hebrew/1954.htm.

5   *Strong's Concordance Online*, s.v. "Yehoshua," accessed June 3, 2016, http://biblehub.com/hebrew/3091.htm.

6   *Strong's Concordance Online*, s.v. "Abram," accessed June 3, 2016, http://biblehub.com/hebrew/87.htm.

7   *Strong's Concordance Online*, s.v. "Abraham," accessed June 3, 2016, http://biblehub.com/hebrew/85.htm.

8   *Strong's Concordance Online*, s.v. "Petros," accessed June 3, 2016, http://biblehub.com/greek/4074.htm.

9   Sally Lloyd-Jones, *The Jesus Storybook Bible* (Grand Rapids, MI: Zonderkidz, 2007), 36.